What's the Score?

What's the Score?

Devotions for Sports Lovers

Rolf E. Aaseng

BAKER BOOK HOUSE
Grand Rapids, Michigan 49506

ISBN: 0-8010-0207-9

Third printing, January 1988

Printed in the United States of America

Contents

Scorekeeping

Love keeps no score of wrongs (1 Cor. 13:5, NEB).

What's the score? Is our side winning? Or are we falling behind?

Both the athlete and fan always want to know who's ahead and by how much. Who is the hero—the winning pitcher, the home-run hitter? And who is the goat—the batter who struck out three times, the fielder who made a fatal error? Whom shall we praise or blame?

When our side ends up with the winning score, it makes our day. When we lose, we rush to decide whose fault it is.

It's not only in sports that we like to keep score. Many of us keep a running total in our minds of the wins and losses in many areas of our lives, to see if we have a better score than others. How often have you made the honor roll and been pleased about beating out your classmates? Are you more popular than your friends? Do you get asked for dates or to parties more often than others? Did you get chosen for the starting team ahead of your mates? Can you recite more Bible verses than anyone else at your church's youth group meeting?

It's natural to want to come out ahead in whatever we do. And when we have a good score, we hope that everyone notices.

When we're losing, it's not so pleasant. Perhaps you didn't get invited to the party, although most of the class was there. Your current heartthrob went on a date with someone else. You not only missed the honor roll, but failed an exam. You sat on the bench throughout the game because you had made a costly mistake.

When we're losing, we make up all kinds of excuses for our failures or try to think of how we can blame someone else for our loss.

We may also keep score in our relationships with others. We count up what people have done for us and respond accordingly. If we interpret the Golden Rule as a sort of trade-off—"You do something for me and I'll reciprocate"—then we have to keep score to make sure we don't get too far ahead or behind. "They gave us an expensive gift; we'll have to give them something nice." "I invited them last time; now it's their turn."

Some of us are also careful to keep track of the mean or harmful things others do to us. "I'll forgive, but I won't forget," you say, meaning that you'll do neither. And then you may begin to plot how you can even the score—how you can pay back the wrong.

God doesn't keep score in these ways—fortunately for us. If he kept such records, our percentage of wins would be most embarrassing. There would be plenty of errors and strikeouts but very few home runs.

God doesn't total up our sins to see how they balance with the good we have done. Oh, he knows about all our errors. But he is willing to forgive—not just once, but again and again.

In fact, he throws away our record book. In its place he starts a new score sheet for each of us. He puts our name on it, but it lists the performance of Jesus—no errors. Christ's perfect record becomes ours. In Christ we are winners every time. "More than conquerors," says Paul.

At the same time, God calls on us to put aside our record keeping on others. "How many times shall I forgive someone?" asked Peter. Not seven times, said Jesus, but "seventy times seven" (Matt. 18:22)—in other words, without limit.

Sure, people sin against you. But don't keep score. Forgive. Wipe out the record of wrongs. For that's how God deals with us.

2

Records Don't Win Games

> . . . forgetting what lies behind and straining forward
> to what lies ahead, I press on toward the goal for the
> prize of the upward call of God in Christ Jesus (Phil.
> 3:13–14).

Press clippings never win ball games. Yesterday's score doesn't count in today's game. At the beginning of every new contest, the score is always nothing to nothing. Even if you set a new conference record your last time out, no one is going to declare you the winner this time unless you put in another superior performance.

Some athletes try to live on their reputations. Because of their past successes, they seem to think they will always be in the winning column without having to try too hard. It doesn't work that way, as many have learned to their sorrow.

If the star of the team finds it too much effort to continue to make that extra effort that won him or her a reputation, games are lost that could have been won. Or the hero of last week's game stops taking batting practice, and soon the hits come less frequently. Or the boxing champ begins to take life easy and neglects training. Before long, some unknown slugger cuts him down.

The world is interested in what you can do today, not what you did last year. A straight-*A* record in high school won't impress your employer if you never come to work on time. The diploma hanging on your wall won't guarantee your employment if you don't do the job correctly.

God is not impressed by your past record either. If past reputation meant anything, the apostle Paul was a shoo-in to be included in God's kingdom: from the best Hebrew family, trained by the most famous rabbi, the top student in his class, most zealous to practice his religion. But impressive as his credentials were, these were not what won him eternal life. No, he said all these apparent qualifications made no difference. Only the love of Christ, creating him a new person every day, qualified Paul for God's family.

If you have had mountaintop religious experiences, rejoice in them. If you have been brought up in a Christian family, praise God. If you were confirmed, attended an inspiring conference, or were president of your youth group, thank God for what you gained. But don't depend on those past experiences, no matter how valuable, for your present standing with God.

A little girl fell out of bed one night. Her explanation of why it happened is a timely warning to athletes and Christians: "I fell asleep too close to where I got in."

God offers us eternal victory, not on the basis of our past performances, but because of the love of Christ.

This goal still lies ahead of us. There is no question about whether Christ can get us there. But it means a day-to-day relationship with him, not just a long-ago entry in the record book.

3

To Be
A Winner

Do you not know that in a race all the runners compete, but only one receives the prize? So run that you may obtain it (I Cor. 9:24).

When you were a little kid, you may have run in a race in which everybody got a prize. In order not to discourage the children, all of them were declared winners. But now that you've grown up you know that's not the way the real world works. When you have a track meet, only the winners get a prize.

Yet some people say, "Everyone will get the prize of salvation. God is love: he won't condemn anybody. We'll all end up in heaven."

The Bible does not support that notion. Instead it describes a selection process by which God forges a nation of his own people. Even among those who were chosen, only a remnant, a small proportion, remain faithful and continue to follow him. Jesus spoke of the narrow gate that leads to life, which only a few find. He told of sheep and goats being separated in the judgment, of some who will be raised to life, while others are raised only to be judged.

Salvation is not given to every person who lives on earth, any more than first prize is awarded to everyone who enters a race. Although God freely provides salvation for us, we need to recognize its importance and take it seriously if it is to be ours.

There are forces that try to keep you from getting the salvation God wants you to reach. Satan, the perennial loser, wants company. False prophets will try to get you off the right track. They want to prevent you from finishing the course that God has put you on. "The prize God offers isn't worth much," they say. "Run in the other direction, after a better prize—like money." They may try to persuade you that it isn't necessary to run the race according to God's directions: "Just lead a good life—do the best you can. Faith in Christ isn't essential." They may tempt you to waste your energies on sinful and selfish activities, rather than concentrating on the goal God has set before you.

But if you lose the race, it's usually your own fault. Like the rabbit in the old fable, if you don't take the race seriously and just loaf along, you'll suddenly discover that it's all over and you're nowhere near the finish line.

God calls us to commit ourselves to following Jesus. So, although Paul points out that "God is at work in you" (Phil. 2:13), he at the same time tells us to work out our own salvation (v. 12). He says that God "will render to every man according to his works: to those who by patience in well-doing seek for glory and honor and immortality, he will give eternal life; but for those who are factious and do not obey the truth, but obey wickedness, there will be wrath and fury" (Rom. 2:6–8).

We need first to recognize that the goal God has set before us is more important than anything else in our lives and then give ourselves wholeheartedly to reaching it.

4

Power
to Last

. . . the race is not to the swift . . . (Eccles. 9:11).

Life is not a 100-yard dash.

It is more like a 10,000-meter test of endurance.

Those who start out like a house afire may not last the distance. In one of his parables, Jesus talked about seed that springs up quickly after it is planted but withers as soon as the sun comes out. Some people are like that. They begin well but wilt when the going becomes difficult.

There's a long road ahead in your life. A good start is of great value, but what really counts is endurance. Finishing high school is a big milestone, but it is only a beginning.

Maybe you've run in a marathon. You didn't really expect to win; all you wanted was to stick it out to the end. In most marathons, everyone who reaches the finish line merits recognition. You don't have to come in first or even in the top ten.

It's that way in the marathon of life, too. Jesus promises, "He who endures to the end will be saved" (Matt. 24:13).

How can we obtain the stamina we need to continue to the end? Endurance depends less on native strength than on proper preparation. Perhaps you have known an athlete with great natural abilities who never amounted to much because he broke the training rules and got out of condition. On the other hand, almost every team includes an average athlete who has trained faithfully and well and is a winner. "Games are won in the training camp," the coaches say. That's where the players get into condition so they can maintain a high level of performance the whole way.

Similarly, our natural abilities do not win a place for us in God's kingdom. Rather, it is the strength that God builds up in us that enables us to complete the course.

Again and again the Bible urges us to make preparations so we can endure what lies ahead. "Be ready," Jesus urged, and he clearly spelled out what difficulties we shall have to face. "In the world you have tribulation . . ." (John 16:33b). "I send you as sheep in the midst of wolves . . ." (Matt. 10:16). "If they persecuted me, they will persecute you . . ." (John 15:21b). You may already have experienced some of these roadblocks.

We prepare for the long haul by making use of the resources available in Christ. He alone can give us the endurance we need. "Apart from me you can do nothing," he said (John 15:5b). But Jesus promises to provide what we need: "Ask and you shall receive." He offers the strength of God's Word and sacraments, power in the working of the Holy Spirit, and encouragement in the companionship of fellow believers. Thus Paul can declare, "I can do all things in [Christ] who strengthens me" (Phil 4:13). And he assures us that God shall supply all our needs (v. 19).

The race of life is long and difficult. We know that already. But God has provided resources that will enable us to endure to the end and reach the goal.

5

One Way

. . . "I am the way, and the truth, and the life; no one comes to the Father, but by me" (John 14:6).

In cross-country races and marathons, the course is clearly marked by flags or other signs. Runners must follow the course that has been laid out. If they go some other route or try to take a shortcut, they are disqualified.

Not long ago someone took a shortcut in the Boston Marathon. But the trick was discovered, and the victory was taken away from the runner who cheated.

The Bible marks out the course of life for us. There is only one way to the goal God has set before us. If we try to get to the finish line by some other way, we disqualify ourselves. If we attempt to find a shortcut, we inevitably get lost.

"I am the way," Jesus said. The way to God's kingdom, to the eternal life he has prepared for us, is through Jesus. There is no other.

Some people say that any route we take is acceptable and will bring us to heaven. "We're all going to

23

the same place," they stubbornly maintain. But Jesus said, "No one comes to the Father, but by me." Peter made this emphatic: ". . . there is no other name under heaven, given among men, by which we must be saved" (Acts 4:12).

Why is Jesus the only way? Because he alone, by his death and resurrection, is able to take away the consequences of the sin that keeps us from God. In the Garden of Gethsemane Jesus asked if there could not be another way. But there was none. He remains the only way to heaven for all of us.

When we have to go to a place where we've never been before—to a new school, a place of possible employment, a strange city—we always feel better if we can go with someone who has been there before. When we face the unknown future, and eventually death, we can do it with more confidence if we go with Jesus. For he has traveled this way before. He went through death's door and returned, demonstrating his victory over it. Now he has gone ahead of us to the new world that awaits us, where he will welcome us to the place he has prepared for us.

Early Christians were called "followers of the way," because in their lives they were following the way Jesus had marked out. Though the way is clearly identified, the Bible warns that not everyone finds it. And some who know of it prefer to try to forge their own way. But they get nowhere.

To those who stay on course, who center their hopes in Jesus and follow his leading, his way leads to the goal. They can say with Paul, "I have fought the good fight, I have finished the race. . . . Henceforth there is laid up for me the crown of righteousness, which the Lord, the righteous judge, will award to me on that Day . . ." (2 Tim. 4:7–8).

On Target

For many who lay claim to it [knowledge] have shot far wide of the faith (I Tim. 6:21, NEB).

We've all met persons who think they know it all. They know better than the teachers what they should study. They can devise better scoring plays than the coach. They confidently start putting together a bicycle or some other complicated device without bothering to read the instructions. They claim more information than any of us on almost any subject.

But, in most cases, it doesn't take long before their claim to superior knowledge turns out to be only hot air. If you want to do something well, rather than trying the first method that occurs to you, you'll be more successful if you learn the right way from someone who really knows.

Target shooting, for example, looks easy, but there are right and wrong ways to go about it. The gun should be held in a certain way. There is a proper way to take aim. The trigger must be squeezed carefully.

Even correct posture is important. When we follow the advice of an expert, we can expect to begin hitting the bull's-eye after a little practice.

But some would-be sharpshooters think they can do it better in their own way. After all, they've seen how it is done in the movies! Why should they go about it as if they were just beginners? But soon they may be wondering why their shots miss the target, while the novice who listened to good advice hits it dead center.

All of us like to do things our own way, whether shooting at a target or gaining entrance into heaven. To admit that the method we have worked out for ourselves isn't any good is humiliating.

Perhaps nothing keeps people from God as much as pride that refuses to acknowledge that our slipshod way of gaining salvation won't work. Many people say, "I lead a good life; I'll be okay." But the Bible says that approach misses the target. It calls on us to stop trying to do things our own way and to listen to what God says.

All people fall short of the glory of God—this is obvious. Thus the Bible directs us to the only way to come to God: God's way, the way of faith. This means first acknowledging our inability to make ourselves good enough for God—the church calls this confessing our sin—and then relying on Christ to forgive. "Repent and believe" is how the biblical preachers often put it.

Until we abandon our pretensions to expertise, our expectations that we can somehow qualify for heaven by what we are or do, God will tell us, "Depart from me; I never knew you—you've missed the target."

But when we listen to God and depend on him to make us what we should be, success is ours. Bull's-eye!

7

Mismatched

For we are not contending against flesh and blood,
but against the principalities, against the powers,
against the world rulers of this present darkness,
against the spiritual hosts of wickedness in the
heavenly places (Eph. 6:12).

Pick on somebody your own size!" We get
angry when we see a high-school student tormenting
a third-grader. It isn't fair!

In sports, too, we complain when we witness a
contest between two people or teams that are ob-
viously mismatched. We expect that teams or individuals that compete should have comparable abilities
and experience. We object to a beginner being forced to
play against a pro.

That is why athletic programs for children are carefully divided by age groups. And boxing matches are
between individuals in the same weight class. When
a promoter rushes an inexperienced fighter into a
bout with an opponent who has a long record of victo-
ries, in an attempt to earn a fast buck, there are loud
criticisms.

By ordinary standards, the Christian is matched against opponents that are clearly out of his or her class. It doesn't look like a fair fight. We are not just competing against other people, but against "principalities, spiritual hosts, powers, rulers"—forces much stronger than any individual. What chance do we have of survival, let alone victory?

But the Bible tells of many mismatches that had surprising results for the apparent underdog. The shepherd boy David conquered the giant professional soldier Goliath. Gideon with a handful of green troops defeated a well-trained army. The Israelite slaves in Egypt overcame the powerful forces of Pharaoh's army.

Such upsets can still happen.

How? The answer is in what onlookers probably regarded as another mismatch: Jesus—"despised and rejected of men; with no beauty that we should desire him"—was pitted against the might of the Jewish religious establishment and the Roman government and ended up a pitiful figure strung out on a cross.

Yet he won! ". . . I have overcome the world," he announced (John 16:33), and his triumph gives the power of victory to his followers, no matter how overwhelmingly the odds may seem to be against us. The good news about his victory is the power of God that is employed on our behalf. It makes each of us "more than conquerors." In fact, we might say the contest is now a mismatch in the other direction—our opponents have no hope of overcoming anyone who has Christ on his or her side.

By ourselves, we are mismatched in our struggle against the forces of evil that assault us in this world.

Alone, we would have no hope. But, with Christ in our corner, the tables are turned. As Martin Luther said, the "right man" is on our side—"and he must win the battle."

A Midnight Wrestling Match

And Jacob was left alone; and a man wrestled with him until the breaking of the day (Gen. 32:24).

Who ever heard of a wrestling match lasting all night?

Yet Jacob wrestled all night. With a man? An angel? God himself? Perhaps the writer himself was not sure. More than a man, surely, for by a single touch he permanently disabled Jacob. Yet Jacob seemed able to hold him to a draw.

What is the meaning of this strange wrestling match?

In his early life, Jacob was a scoundrel. He shamelessly cheated his brother, Esau, out of his inheritance and wasn't above lying to his old and blind father, Isaac. He outmaneuvered his equally crafty uncle, Laban. Jacob lived by his wits and always seemed able to come out on top.

Do you know someone like that—always able to turn things to his or her advantage? Sometimes you may wish you could operate in that way—though you know it isn't right.

But all his cleverness had not won Jacob the security he wanted, and now he was in danger of losing everything his wits and cunning had won him. He was returning to his home country, from which he had fled after he had cheated Esau. Esau was waiting for him with four hundred men, no doubt to carry out his earlier threat to kill Jacob.

Jacob did everything he could think of to get out of this scrape, probably figuring that if worse came to worst, he could at least save his own skin. He sent gifts to Esau. He divided his entourage into small groups. He let his wives and children go ahead of him. Thus he found himself alone with God on the eve of the fateful meeting with the brother he had wronged.

Did Jacob finally realize it takes more than cleverness to be victorious in life? Was he ready to acknowledge that his human resources weren't enough for the really important battles of life? Did his midnight wrestling bout make him admit he needed help from someone stronger than himself?

However it came about, he finally in desperation called to God for a blessing. When he reached the end of his rope, he at least knew where to turn for help.

The odd thing is that God responds even to such last-resort appeals. In God's place we would probably say, "Let them get the fate they deserve." But God isn't like us. Even if we have been fighting against him all our lives, when we finally admit we have beaten ourselves and need his help, he is ready to forgive. He gives us blessings he has been waiting to give us all along.

Thus, after his wrestling match with God, Jacob's meeting with Esau was a time of reconciliation, not war. And Jacob, for all his faults, is now remembered as one of the leaders of God's people.

That God would forgive and bless a knave like Jacob assures us that no matter what our past has been, when we finally admit our need and turn to the Lord, he is waiting to receive us. For he is a God who saves sinners.

9

Strong Man

When he [Samson] came to Lehi, the Philistines came shouting to meet him; and the Spirit of the LORD came mightily upon him, and the ropes which were on his arms became as flax that has caught fire, and his bonds melted off his hands (Judg. 15:14).

What a great contest we would have if Samson could compete with the champion weight lifters of today! Could even Olympic medalists carry away a city gate, destroy a thousand soldiers with the jawbone of an ass, or tear down a temple with their bare hands? These feats have led us to think of Samson as the world's strongest man.

For all his strength, Samson was not the sort of person we like to hold up as a model of behavior. He disregarded the wishes of his parents and broke the commands of God. He was brutally vengeful. He consorted with prostitutes. And he surely wasn't very smart. Although Delilah twice betrayed him to the Philistines, he still confided to her the secret of his strength, which enabled them to capture him.

Yet the biblical writer seems to feel the story of Samson is worth telling. Why?

It is clear that Samson's remarkable strength was dependent on his relationship with God. When he betrayed God's confidence in him, he became weak. Physical strength and other desirable human qualities have their source in God. Do we sometimes boast of our strength or other abilities—or at least secretly feel proud of what we can do—instead of thanking God for what he has given us?

The biblical account also suggests that the gifts of God, in this case physical strength, are intended to be used to carry out God's purposes rather than to bring glory to ourselves. Samson's role and the purpose of his strength were to relieve the oppression of the Israelites by the Philistines. For what purpose do you use the abilities that God has given you? "As each has received a gift," says Peter, "employ it for one another . . ." (1 Peter 4:10).

We also can learn from the story that God can use people with very obvious faults to work for him. Samson is not the only example of this truth. God uses sinful people to carry out his plans. Of course—what other kind is there?

The story of Samson should keep us from excusing ourselves from doing God's work because we think we aren't good enough. When God has a job for us to do, he gives us the ability to do it. We may not be Samsons, but God provides the strength we need to do what he wants us to do.

10

Following the Rules

An athlete is not crowned unless he competes according to the rules (2 Tim. 2:5).

The car streaked across the finish line well ahead of all competitors. As the crowd cheered, the driver was acclaimed the winner. But wait a minute! After a pause, the judge made an announcement: the apparent winner was disqualified. Because he had broken a rule, his victory was taken from him and given to another racer.

This happened in a major auto race. But we all know of something like it. A touchdown is called back because a player had been "holding." An athlete is barred from competition because he or she had taken forbidden drugs. A new record is erased from the books because the victor had used illegal equipment.

In any competition, if you break the rules, you'll never be a winner, no matter how much better you are than the other players.

This is true in the race of life, too. Apparent winners are sometimes disqualified because they have not followed the rules. They may have been leaders in the church youth group. Perhaps they could pray beautifully in public and recite Bible verses nonstop. Yet they may still hear the verdict, "Disqualified; you didn't follow the rules."

What are these rules that must be followed? Some people once put the question to Jesus this way: "What must we do, to be doing the works of God?" Jesus answered with what might be called the basic rule of Christianity: "This is the work of God, that you believe in him whom he has sent" (John 6:29). To be a winner in God's sight, believe in Christ.

What about the other rules—God's laws?

The Ten Commandments are good rules to live by, and they make our lives better. But they don't make us winners, for the simple reason that we can't keep them perfectly. Only Christ can do that. We qualify as winners on the basis of what Christ has done for us.

But belief in Christ implies a commitment to live for him. That's what the apostle Paul is talking about when he speaks of rules. To say we believe in Jesus, yet then act in ways that violate his will for us, shows we really don't believe. And to pretend to have faith when we don't is the surest way to be disqualified from entering God's kingdom. So Paul says he practices self-discipline in his life, "lest after preaching to others I myself should be disqualified" (1 Cor. 9:27b).

But we don't have to live in constant worry that our sinfulness will keep us away from God's goal. For the God who sets the standards is loving and powerful. He has made us winners by bringing us to Christ. His grace will continue to keep us victorious through our faith in him: ". . . he who began a good work in you will bring it to completion at the day of Jesus Christ" (Phil. 1:6).

A Miss Is as Good as a Mile

. . . some have missed the mark as regards the faith (1 Tim. 6:21).

"Strike three!"

When you miss the ball after two strikes, you're out. It doesn't matter how hard you swing, how faithfully you've trained, or how sincere you are. It makes no difference if you miss by just a fraction of an inch. If you miss, you're out.

The most common word for sin in the Bible means simply "to miss the mark." That doesn't sound so serious; for who can help missing occasionally? The best batters sometimes strike out. No one expects even an *A* student in school to come through with the right answer for every question.

Yet to miss is to sin. It technically disqualifies us from God's kingdom—for God, who is perfect, demands perfection in those who are to live with him.

We may come close. But close isn't enough. Seventy-five or even ninety-nine percent isn't passing in this case. Just as the slightest deviation—only a fraction of an inch—from the course in a space vehicle sends the craft thousands of miles from its target, so the least imperfection in our lives results in our being unfit for God's kingdom.

If the pitcher misses the plate, it doesn't matter if it is a half-inch or a yard; it's a ball and counts against him. So James says that "whoever keeps the whole law but fails in one point has become guilty of all of it" (James 2:10).

What can cause you to miss? Perhaps you don't take the situation seriously enough. You think, "I can hit this guy"—and the pitcher turns out to have more on the ball than you expected. In the same way, underestimating evil can cause you to miss—to sin.

Perhaps you were expecting something else, like a batter looking for a fast ball who gets a change-up instead. Forces of evil try to trick you so that you're unprepared for what comes. Temptation is most effective when least expected.

Maybe it is lack of practice; your "batting eye" is rusty because you haven't kept up your faith training. Perhaps it is a lack of concentration; you aren't taking your faith seriously enough.

Underlying all the reasons for missing is the fact that none of us is perfect. Thus a flawless performance is beyond us. We're bound to miss.

But, even so, we are not automatically out. We have a pinch hitter whose record is unequalled: Jesus Christ. He has acted on our behalf. We may miss, occasionally or often. But, in Christ, we always score.

12

Ready, Aim . . .

But as for you, man of God, shun all this; aim at righteousness, godliness, faith, love, steadfastness, gentleness (1 Tim. 6:11).

The shooters hurried to inspect their targets. One of the marksmen, to his great chagrin, found not a single hole in his target. All of his shots had missed by a wide margin!

What was wrong with his gun? Or was he too near-sighted to see clearly? Maybe he hadn't learned the proper technique. The group finally concluded there was only one reasonable explanation: he had been aiming at the wrong target!

In contrast, Babe Ruth once pointed to the fence, then hit the next pitch over that fence for a home run. He knew what he was aiming at.

What you aim at in life makes a great difference in what happens to you. Perhaps you won't always hit the target you are shooting at. But it surely helps to aim in the right direction!

This is true in spiritual matters, too. "You will seek me and find me; when you seek me with all your heart," says the Lord through Jeremiah (29:13). But if we are not even seeking him, how can we hope to find God?

Some individuals finish high school and then wonder what they should do. They have no aim in life. Sometimes they even go through college without having any purpose in mind. As a result they rarely amount to much, and their lives never satisfy themselves or anyone else.

Most people, however, do have an aim. They may not have formulated it in words, but they devote most of their energies and time to a specific long-term goal.

What are you aiming at? To make money? To get power or become famous? To be an expert in the use of computers?

Aims such as these, though not necessarily wrong, are not enough. Money won't last. Those who attain power will one day lose it, since fame depends on the whims of public opinion, which has a short memory. Technical expertise is eventually outdated.

Instead of such short-lived goals, the Bible encourages us to aim at an assortment of worthy targets: righteousness, godliness, faith, love, steadfastness, gentleness. Are such aims important enough to devote our lives to them? Many would say no. The Bible makes it clear, however, that God's measurement standards are often the reverse of the world's. Eventually, when all that the world considers valuable has disintegrated, God's values will still stand. "The grass withers, and the flower falls, but the word of the Lord abides for ever" (1 Peter 1:24b).

If we aim at what God considers important, his promise is that through his power we will attain goals beyond our wildest expectations. Jesus told us to "seek first [God's] kingdom and his righteousness, and all these things shall be yours as well" (Matt. 6:33).

13

One Objective

Make love your aim . . . (1 Cor. 14:1).

Someday I'm going to the Olympics." Many young athletes have this as their ultimate goal. The one thing above all else that they want to accomplish in life is to compete in the Olympics. All the rigorous training they go through and every competition they enter are thought of as steps toward achieving that objective.

Most athletes have such an aim. Some hope to win, or at least to play, at Wimbledon or in the U.S. Open or a Bowl game. Others will be satisfied to make their school's starting team. Or the aim may be simply to have enough stamina to run an entire marathon. Whatever it is, this ambition is always in the athlete's thinking and motivates him or her to continue efforts until the goal is reached.

What's your aim? What do you want most to happen in your Christian life? According to the Bible, the most worthy objective for a Christian is to live a life of love.

Jesus summarized all the commandments by saying we should love God and our neighbor. James says love covers a multitude of sins (1 Peter 4:8). Paul told the Corinthians that the greatest of God's gifts, the greatest Christian trait, is love (1 Cor. 13:13). The way we demonstrate that we are followers of Christ is by showing love to others. If any one word comes close to summarizing what God wants us to be, it is love.

But when we try to fulfill this aim of love, we are often disappointed. As some liturgies put it, we must confess that "we have not loved God with our whole heart, nor our neighbors as ourselves." What then?

We need to go to the source of love: God. ". . . for God is love," says John (1 John 4:8). Our ability to love, in fact even our desire to love others, comes from him: "In this is love, not that we loved God but that he loved us . . ." (1 John 4:10). God has shown us in Jesus what it is to love: "Greater love has no man than this, to lay down his life for his friends" (John 15:13). By his love, God inspires us to love and, more important, makes it possible for us to do so: "We love because he first loved us" (1 John 4:19).

Love in the biblical sense is not an emotion that suddenly hits us out of the blue. It is not a feeling that leaves us breathless or weak-kneed. It is a deliberate decision to act in ways that benefit someone else.

The more we become aware of God's love for us, the more we are motivated and enabled to reflect that love to others. God's love fills us, with the result that more and more our lives come closer to reaching our ultimate aim. We are thereby enabled to love God and our fellow humans in a way that fulfills God's purpose and ours and gives glory to him.

Fight

Fight the good fight of the faith . . . (1 Tim. 6:12).

Wanna fight?" goes the challenge.

Most of us would probably rather not. But, like it or not, if we are followers of Christ, we're involved in a fight to the finish. Although some Christians are so opposed to war and violence that they object to the militant language of such hymns as "Onward, Christian Soldiers," the unpleasant fact is that we are under attack from evil forces around and within us. They intend to destroy us. If we don't resist, they will succeed.

These enemies try to bluff us into joining them, arguing that the majority is on their side and they are bound to win. They try to overwhelm us by a series of disappointments so that we give up in despair. Or, by promising great rewards, they try to bribe us into throwing the fight.

They may mislead us into thinking we're winning an easy victory—then wham! When our defenses are down, they attack where we least expect. They try to trick us into making foolish mistakes or ignoring God's instructions. They stir up differences among us so we will fight one another.

It's a real battlefield out there. You won't survive if you're content with a halfhearted or part-time defense. A couple of hours in church on Sunday morning is not enough to ward off this enemy. It calls for a continuing total effort. "You shall love the Lord your God with *all* your heart, and with *all* your soul, and with *all* your mind," said Jesus. Following Christ is to be the top priority in your life. Anything less is bound to fail.

Once you realize you're in a fight, you'll be on the lookout for the enemies' tricks. You can avoid getting into situations in which you can easily be led into sin. You will arm yourself with the defensive resources God provides: his Word and promises, prayer, the sacraments. You will ally yourself with other believers, so you can fight together. Above all, you will keep in constant contact with God and rely on his power.

Ours is a fight of faith. Our hope for success comes not from our fighting ability but in our commitment to Jesus, the Champion who fights for us. "This is the victory that overcomes the world, our faith" (1 John 5:4)—faith in Christ, who has already defeated the enemy and invites us to share his triumph.

Martin Luther sang:

> A mighty fortress is our God,
> A bulwark never failing;
> Our helper he, amid the flood
> Of mortal ills prevailing. . . .
> Did we in our own strength confide
> Our striving would be losing;
> Were not the right Man on our side,

The Man of God's own choosing.
Dost ask who that may be?
Christ Jesus, it is he;
Lord Sabaoth his Name,
From age to age the same,
And he must win the battle.

15

Obstacle Course

> . . . we rejoice in our sufferings, knowing that
> suffering produces endurance (Rom. 5:3).

Can you imagine anyone enjoying an obstacle course, or rejoicing in the rigors of a football training camp? Most of us would rather do without such dubious pleasures.

We know, of course, that such demanding exercises are for our own good. They build up our strength, our endurance, our agility. Then, when the big game comes and the players are beginning to tire, we will be able to give an extra effort and win.

Defeat or victory often depends on how strenuous—actually how unpleasant—our training has been. As the saying goes: "No pain, no gain."

Therefore, if we decide that in order to achieve our purpose we have to endure some arduous exercises, we grit our teeth and go through them. But no one pretends it is enjoyable. We are glad when it's over.

Everyone's life includes some suffering and unpleasantness. We may wonder why, and perhaps human beings cannot find an entirely satisfactory answer. But we can discover that like the ordeal of training camps, life's difficulties can be blessings that have beneficial results for us.

What kind of blessings? Peter says the difficulties we meet refine or purify our faith, as fire purifies gold ore. James says the outcome of trials is that we become perfect and complete, lacking nothing. Paul says we rejoice in suffering because of the benefits it brings: endurance, character, hope—centered in God's love.

Did your parents ever punish you when you were a child? If so, you certainly didn't enjoy it. But, as you grew older, you began to realize that such discipline was actually necessary. It helped you to tell right from wrong and steered you away from harmful habits and dangerous situations. The writer of Hebrews says suffering is like the disciplining a parent carries out with children. He observes, "For the moment all discipline seems painful rather than pleasant; later it yields the peaceful fruit of righteousness to those who have been trained by it" (Heb. 12:11).

When we suffer, Peter says, we should remember Jesus. He suffered too—unjustly. Yet how necessary it was! Without that suffering everything would be lost for all of us. Christ's suffering was redemptive; it saves us from condemnation.

Our suffering, too, can be beneficial. It can build character in us. It can make possible some good results for others. All of us, for example, profit from the difficult life the pioneers in our country endured.

Don't be surprised by suffering; it is to be expected in the kind of world we live in. But God can use our difficulties to make us better people. Trust him to do so.

16

The Uniform

Put on the whole armor of God . . . (Eph. 6:11).

Suppose some visitors from outer space saw your school's football team dressed for a big game. What would they think? Wouldn't they likely conclude, "These are warriors getting ready for battle. See how much armor they wear!"?

Of course the uniform is armor of a sort. The various items of equipment have been developed to protect players from injury. To play football without using this "armor" exposes you to possible serious harm.

Christians, too, have armor: equipment provided by God to protect us from the frequently violent onslaughts of the enemy. The fields of church history are littered with bodies of persons who failed to use the available protection.

Paul's description of the Christian's armor does sound somewhat like a football uniform. For example, he said to "put on the helmet of salvation" (v. 17). The head, the center of our thinking, is vulnerable to serious injury. Our thinking can be damaged so that it leads us to oppose God. The protection we need is not a larger brain or greater wisdom; what will keep us safe is the salvation God has prepared for us. His saving power helps to safeguard our minds so that they work for our good as he intends.

Truth and righteousness protect our bodies. Truth, revealed to us by God, helps us to know what is good and what is bad. It shows us what is important in life so we don't waste our efforts in useless or harmful actions. "The breastplate of righteousness," also given by God, defends us from the destructive results of sin. If it were not for the righteousness of Christ, which is given to us, we all would have been taken out of the contest long ago. But, protected by his righteousness, we are enabled to overcome what would otherwise destroy us.

Paul speaks of shoes, too, as a part of the Christian's uniform, describing them as "the equipment of the gospel of peace" (v. 15). The gospel, the good news of what Christ has done for us, enables us to stand firm in the face of disappointments and failures. We even dare to go on the offensive against evil.

With the protective armor God supplies, we are safe, no matter how strong the opposition. Though there may be temporary setbacks, as long as we remain under God's care, nothing can do us permanent harm.

Furthermore, as we spread the message of peace through Christ, his Spirit guides our efforts and assures us that our activities will be worthwhile.

No matter what opposition we face in life, Christ's armor enables us to carry out God's purpose and to remain standing until he wins the final victory for us.

17

The Thrill of Running

. . . the sun . . . like a strong man runs its course with joy (Ps. 19:4–5).

Do you like to run—to race—to go jogging? Many people find running to be exhilarating. It involves not only the excitement of competing with others, or the possibility of winning a medal. Running itself provides a thrill.

Champion racers often say they are competing with themselves—challenging themselves to do better than the average person, but also testing their ability to improve each time they go out. To be able to get a good performance from our body, to exert ourselves to the limit, to stimulate our body through vigorous exercise—all of this does give a good feeling.

Of course, if this is to be the result, you have to be in shape. Your running cannot be just an occasional spur-of-the-moment activity. Your muscles must be built up so they can respond to the demands you make on them. To run well you must keep at it. This is part of the thrill: to see how you can build up your body as you continue to make the effort.

It can be equally exhilarating to live in our world today—to meet and overcome the challenges that come to us every day. Many people, however, don't experience life as a thrill, but rather more as a threat. The difference may be whether we are in shape— whether we are prepared to respond successfully to the various trials and crises.

For the Christian, keeping in shape means maintaining daily contact with the source of our strength, Christ himself, through prayer and reflection on his words. We need to recognize our limitations and learn to rely on the power of God.

In addition, it is helpful to associate with other believers so we can give each other mutual encouragement. None of us can conquer the world alone. Only with God's help can we succeed and experience the thrill of overcoming difficulties.

But when we have allowed the power of God to get us into condition, facing the trials of life in this world can become an exciting adventure. So James says, "Count it all joy, my brethren, when you meet various trials, for you know that the testing of your faith produces steadfastness" (1:2).

When we rely on the power of God and look toward the future he has prepared for us, the difficulties of this world can become challenges that call forth the best in us and lead us through trials to eternal life with our Lord.

18

Stumbling

... if you run, you will not stumble (Prov. 4:12).

A small pebble. A loose shoelace. A shout from the sidelines. All are insignificant in themselves. Yet such small things can cause a runner to stumble and lose the big race.

Sometimes we stumble in our Christian lives, too, and the results can be equally disastrous.

Usually the cause of stumbling is a very minor thing, like a little stone on the track. Someone makes a nasty remark to you; you fail an exam; no one says thanks when you've done a good deed. Nothing very important. But such things can make us stumble.

Friends have become enemies; churches have split; wars have been started; faith has been lost—because of overreacting to incidents that ordinarily would be forgotten in a few weeks. Before you get upset by such a pebble on the track ask yourself, "What difference will this make a hundred years from now?"

The cause of stumbling could be compared to a faulty shoe. Paul tells us to wear the shoes of the gospel of peace. If our steps are directed by the gospel, if we have God's peace in our lives and are concerned to spread it to others, we are not as likely to stumble over incidents that could otherwise cause friction and unrest.

Most often the cause of stumbling is that we fail to keep our eyes on the track ahead. We look around—to see if we're ahead of others, to acknowledge the cheers or boos of the crowd—and we stumble and fall. If we keep our attention focused on Jesus, the chances of stumbling are diminished.

Christ is able and willing to guide us in ways that will reduce the probability of stumbling. "He is able to keep you from falling . . ." writes Jude (v. 24).

If you stumble in a footrace, other runners will pass you and you most likely will lose the race. But if you stumble in the race of life, you haven't lost everything. You get another opportunity, a chance to recover and go on to win.

For when we stumble, Christ is there to pick us up and set us on the right path again. John assures us that "if any one does sin, we have an advocate with the Father, Jesus Christ the righteous" (1 John 2:16).

Let us do our best to avoid stumbling. But if we fall, Christ sends us on our way again with an encouraging word: "Neither do I condemn you; go and do not sin again" (John 8:11b).

19

Overconfidence

Pride goes before destruction, and a haughty spirit before a fall (Prov. 16:18).

Have you ever gone into a game against a weak opponent and been so confident of victory that you didn't take it seriously? But the supposedly weak opponent turned out to be tougher than anyone thought, and you suffered a humiliating defeat!

Overconfidence in sports—or in life—is costly and dangerous. When we convince ourselves that we are more capable than we really are, or when we underestimate the opposition so that we fail to make adequate preparations and don't exert ourselves to the fullest, we suffer our most embarrassing defeats.

Among biblical examples the most famous is Peter. When Jesus foretold that all the disciples would desert him and singled out Peter for a special warning, that disciple vehemently insisted, "Even though they all fall away, I will not" (Mark 14:29). Yet only hours later a servant girl frightened all the bravado out of him so that he denied even knowing Jesus. If Peter hadn't been so sure of himself—if he had admitted the possibility of personal failure—would he have been better able to remain true when the test came?

When we are especially sure of ourselves, we seem to be particularly vulnerable to failure. The Bible thus warns us, "Let any one who thinks that he stands take heed lest he fall" (1 Cor. 10:12).

In spiritual matters the reason for this is that we face an opponent who is much stronger than we are, although it may not always look that way. If we are to prevail, God must come to our aid. When we ignore the help God promises and go into the tests alone, disaster follows. As God says through Obadiah, "The pride of your heart has deceived you . . ." (v. 3).

Thus Paul can say, "When I am weak, then I am strong" (2 Cor. 12:10b). When he remembers his weakness and relies on Christ's strength, victory is his. Then he can assert, "I can do all things in him who strengthens me" (Phil. 4:13).

We like to think we can always be a winner, like Superman. But that's not the way it is. Winners we are, but only in the strength of God.

"Such is the confidence that we have through Christ toward God," writes Paul—"Not that we are sufficient of ourselves to claim anything as coming from us; our sufficiency is from God" (2 Cor. 3:4–5).

20

Room for Improvement

Not that I have already obtained this or am already perfect; but I press on to make it my own, because Christ Jesus has made me his own (Phil. 3:12).

Perhaps you have heard a sports announcer exclaim, "We've seen a performance here today that will never be equalled!" Or after your school hero has had a particularly good day, you have enthusiastically told a friend, "I'll bet his record will never be broken!"

People who make such statements usually live long enough to learn that they were wrong. Records are constantly being broken. Best performances are sooner or later surpassed.

Knowing this, good athletes are rarely satisfied to rest on past laurels, but are constantly trying to improve. When their record is broken, they want to do it themselves. When one champion was asked, "What was your best race?" he replied, "My next one."

Anyone, athlete or not, who thinks he or she has reached the top and it's impossible to rise higher is only showing a lack of experience. The high-school graduate who thinks he or she knows it all is in for some painful lessons. Experience teaches us that perfection is not compatible with humanity; there is always someone who can improve on what we have done.

Some Christians think they have run the perfect race—that they have attained the level of perfection God requires and need not worry any more about sin. The more mature realize how naive and dangerous such a belief is. Scripture warns often against thinking too highly of oneself, and Jesus says that "whoever exalts himself will be humbled . . ." (Matt. 23:12).

We all have a long way to go in Christian living; none of us has it made. In fact, we are included in God's kingdom not because we have reached the standard of performance God demands, but rather because he is merciful. We haven't met even the minimum qualifications, yet our God—out of love and pity—accepts us nonetheless.

All of us would like to be perfect, and we do our best to improve. But it seems the closer we get to the goal in Christian living, the more we realize how much further we have to go. We see our imperfections more and more clearly. They were there all the time, of course, but they were invisible to us. Thus the great missionary Paul says, "and I am the foremost of sinners" (1 Tim. 1:15b). We might not agree, but he meant it.

But Paul did not give up. He simply learned to depend more and more on Christ. For he knew that Christ can turn our imperfections into perfection and bring us safely to the goal of God's kingdom.

21

Practice Makes Perfect

> . . . Train yourself in godliness; for while bodily training is of some value, godliness is of value in every way, as it holds promise for the present life and also for the life to come (I Tim. 4:7–8).

If your idea of exercise is to get out of the easy chair to change channels from one football game to another, you may think this passage is for you. According to some translations, Paul seems to be saying that bodily exercise is of no real value.

That isn't quite what he says, of course. And when we remember the stonings, beatings, shipwrecks, and other hardships that Paul survived in his ministry, it is obvious that he must have kept himself in pretty good condition. In these verses he is simply maintaining that if physical training is of value—and he doesn't deny that—spiritual training is infinitely more valuable.

Whether or not we actually go jogging or do push-ups, most of us will agree that physical exercise is a good idea. It makes us feel better and keeps us healthy so we may have the strength to meet the demands of daily life in our world.

But isn't spiritual health just as necessary? Considering all the challenges we face as we try to follow Christ, we surely need all the strength we can get.

How do we go about training ourselves in godliness? By developing and practicing those activities that help us to be what God intends us to be. Spiritual strength doesn't come automatically, any more than strong muscles are developed by lying in bed or watching someone else exercise.

The source of our strength is Christ. Paul says, "I can do all things in him [Christ] who strengthens me." Thus spiritual training starts by maintaining a relationship of faith in Christ—by constantly reminding ourselves of his words and promises and recalling what he has done for us. This enables his Spirit to enter us and build us up.

The Bible further urges us to watch and pray so as to avoid temptation, to practice hospitality, to show love to one another. We are encouraged to keep in contact with God through prayer and worship and to find ways of serving other people in his name. These faith-building activities build and enhance our spiritual health and endurance.

However, let's not fool ourselves by supposing that by these practices we will make ourselves godly. Only God's working in us can make us what he wants us to be. On the other hand, the less we are engaged in spiritual training, the more difficult it becomes to remain true to God.

In faith, as in other aspects of life, practice makes perfect.

22

Self-Control

Every athlete exercises self-control in all things . . .
(1 Cor. 9:25).

Every champion needs two qualities. The first is natural physical ability. The second is a mental attitude: a commitment to discipline and self-control. The latter approach makes the difference between an ordinary performer and a real star. The person with great talent alone may have some spectacular successes, but unless there is accompanying dedication that governs all of life, he or she soon fades from the scene.

The real champion trains—not just occasionally, but continually. In pursuit of ongoing excellence, long hours are spent in practice—time that could otherwise be spent in what most of us would consider more enjoyable activities. At all times the champion exercises self-control, giving up some luxuries in order to keep in top condition. Most people are unwilling to give so much of themselves toward a goal. The one who does is the champ.

You've seen this yourself, and not just in athletics. The lead guitarist skips a party to work on some tricky chords. The student who gets the best marks rejects the temptation to have fun when there is studying to be done. In every field—sports, art, music, craftsmanship, business—the person who is willing to sacrifice some of the common indulgences of life in order to pursue his or her vision is the one who gets to the top. The biblical writer recognized this truth when he advised, "Whatever your hand finds to do, do it with your might . . ." (Eccles. 9:10).

The application to Christian life may not be apparent. After all, we are not saved by following rules. There are no super-Christians. Yet we are constantly called upon not to be misled by the values and priorities of the world, but to concentrate on God's will. Jesus urges us to deny ourselves so we can be true to God. Christians give up some practices, even pleasures that others enjoy, if they would keep them from something that is more important.

If you've tried it, you know that such self-control is difficult. But it is possible because it is among the gifts God has given us. Paul lists it as one of the gifts of the Spirit: "God did not give us a spirit of timidity but a spirit of power and love and self-control" (2 Tim. 1:7).

It is not your self-control that wins the prize; salvation and eternal life are given to us by God. But those who exercise discipline in their lives, refusing to give in to the temptation not to take religion so seriously, find daily life more satisfying and fulfilling. And they give glory to God.

23

Weights

> . . . let us also lay aside every weight, and sin which clings so closely, and let us run with perseverance the race that is set before us (Heb. 12:1).

If you are a runner, you may have sometimes fastened weights on your legs when you go on practice runs in training. It's a good idea, even though it makes your practice session much more strenuous. It builds up your leg muscles. And later on, when you run without the weights in a race, it seems that you can almost fly!

But how foolish it would be to tie weights on your legs when you are about to run a race! It would be like tying one hand behind your back in a boxing or tennis match. If the match means nothing, or if the competition is so weak that it offers no real challenge, it might not make any difference. But in any real contest it would be disastrous.

In the race of life the stakes are high and the opposition is strong. This is no time for fooling around. Yet there are some who in effect tie weights on their legs, which causes them to lose out.

What do we mean by weights? The writer of Hebrews equates them with sin. Any sin—any disobedience against God's will—is a hindrance in the Christian life.

It might be self-centeredness or selfishness. Or gossiping about your classmates. Or looking down on those who are different from you in color or customs. Excusing your moral lapses by saying everybody does it. Spending your leisure time in questionable activities with people who aren't concerned with their relationship to God. Lacking concern for people in need.

From a similar point of view, persons who allow such sins in their lives might be compared to athletes who report for training overweight. Because they have overindulged and aren't in condition, they are sluggish and ineffective. Someone else in better shape will take their place, and they will be ousted from the team.

Failure to take sin seriously, or ignoring the deadly effects it has in our lives, leads to our being disqualified from God's team and meeting defeat.

Christ has taken away the weights of our sin. Let us not insist on carrying them again.

24

Shadow-Boxing

Well, I do not run aimlessly, I do not box as one beating the air (1 Cor. 9:26).

You'll never win the world title by shadow-boxing. Nor will you ever win a race by pedaling a stationary bicycle or running in place.

Such exercises can be worthwhile. A boxer can develop skills by shadow-boxing. Running in place can build stamina and muscle. For many reasons, it may be good or even necessary to practice in somewhat artificial circumstances.

But this kind of training is meant to prepare an athlete for something else: a real contest against live opponents. It isn't an end in itself. If we never get beyond the practice room to apply the skills we have learned there, we have gained nothing.

You may dazzle onlookers with your fancy footwork, but you'll never defeat anyone unless you show what you can do in the ring. You may be able to run as fast as a cheetah, but if you only run on a treadmill, you won't win any prizes. The training is for a purpose.

Of course it's more comfortable to stay in the practice room. You may be defeated or get hurt if you venture out to use what you've learned. Thus, in another field, there are actually some people who find the school environment so pleasant that they become perpetual students. They go from one school to another, learning all kinds of interesting and even useful things, but never putting them to any practical use.

Do you suppose there are Christians like that? People who may delight in arguing about theology or who like to dream about how they might overcome evil? But they never want to leave the retreat center or other isolated corner to see if their ideas will work in the real world. They may look and sound good inside the walls of the church, but they are of no value to the kingdom of God. Learning the Ten Commandments, giving testimonies, or passing fine-sounding resolutions are meaningless exercises if we never apply them in our daily life.

Our spiritual training is meant to get us ready for action. God provides resources to strengthen us, not simply for our personal satisfaction, but to accomplish his purposes in the world.

The real fight is not against empty air. There is a solid enemy waiting to deliver a knockout blow. This enemy must be confronted and defeated. It cannot be done in the practice room.

Let us prepare ourselves by all the means we can. But then let us leave the training room and go out into the arena of life to use what we have learned in the tasks God has waiting for us.

25

When You Falter

You were running well; who hindered you from obeying the truth? (Gal. 5:7).

The runner seemed well on the way to victory. She was leading the pack by several lengths. Then she began falling behind the others. Eventually she ran off the track and didn't finish the race.

We occasionally see something like this happen in a race. What is the reason? Sometimes the cause is an injury: a misstep resulting in a sprain, a muscle spasm. Perhaps a shoe came off or got loose. Occasionally the runner was pushed or crowded by a competitor.

At other times there seems to be no explanation. The runner just stumbles or breaks his or her stride. An explanation may be given: "I lost my concentration."

The same thing happens in life. You may have a friend who seems to be maturing well as a Christian, growing in faith daily and acting in kindness to others. Then, suddenly or gradually, the situation changes. Your friend loses interest in worship, Bible reading, or associating with other Christians. Obeying God's will is no longer of supreme importance. Discouragement, cynicism, and even despair take over.

There are many causes for such a change. The devil or his agents may interfere, exerting pressure or offering temptations in an effort to bring about disobedience to God. A particularly trying situation may develop: a failure, a loss or disappointment, or some other setback. Like a stone in one's shoe, it affects one's whole life.

But more often the cause is inner. We falter because our concentration is broken; God no longer is at the center of our existence. Something else seems more important. Our resolve to obey God and follow Christ is shaken. Faith weakens and sometimes disappears.

The Bible often warns against such a development. After reminding his readers of how the Israelites had failed God, Paul says this should be a warning to us. "Let anyone who thinks that he stands," he says, "take heed lest he fall" (1 Cor. 10:12). Jesus told his disciples, "Watch and pray that you may not enter into temptation . . ." (Matt. 26:41).

But failure is not inevitable. Jesus assures us that no one shall snatch his people out of his hand. Paul asserts, "God is faithful, and he will not let you be tempted beyond your strength, but with the temptation will also provide the way of escape, that you may be able to endure it" (1 Cor. 10:13b).

It is God's strength, however, that keeps us faithful. Problems come when we think we are able to obey God's will without his help. But when we remain in a relationship of trust in God, we can say with the apostle: ". . . I know whom I have believed, and I am sure that he is able to guard until that Day what has been entrusted to me" (2 Tim. 1:12).

26

The Cheering Section

Therefore, since we are surrounded by so great a cloud of witnesses, let us also lay aside every weight, and sin which clings so closely, and let us run with perseverance the race that is set before us, looking to Jesus the pioneer and perfecter of our faith . . . (Heb. 12:1–2).

Have you noticed that your school team usually does better when playing on the home field? That's largely because of the vocal support of the fans in the stands. When you as a player hear how all your friends are shouting their encouragement and know they are depending on you to bring victory to their cause, you can't help but put forth extra effort. That added push often provides the margin of victory.

Christians have the advantage of a home crowd, too. Those who have lived before us in the faith might be pictured as now sitting in the stands, urging us on. Of course we do not know whether those who have departed from this life are aware of what is going on here on earth. But we can be sure they are anticipating the completion of God's purpose in his creation, looking forward to our joining them and expecting us to be successful.

In addition, as we learn how believers in the past have remained faithful in difficult situations, we are motivated to follow their example. Maybe you, too, have been inspired to live more wholeheartedly for Christ by the example of one of God's saints.

Furthermore, we have the backing of our teammates: our fellow Christians in the world. Many, especially in times of great stress, have experienced the reality of this backing. Supportive words and prayers, encouraging acts of aid, and the knowledge that others are concerned and praying often enable us to survive the difficulties of life. This strengthening fellowship of the church on earth is a sample of the relationship that will characterize heaven.

Among those cheering us on is one who does more than simply encourage us. This is Jesus, who doesn't just remain in the heavenly stands but comes down on the field to work with us through the Holy Spirit, whom he promised to give to all who believe.

Jesus is working for us from the other side, too. In the councils of God he is not only cheering for us, but actually providing strength. He "always lives to make intercession for us," drawing us nearer to God.

With such support, we are assured of victory.

27

Tests

Blessed is the man who endures trial, for when he has stood the test he will receive the crown of life which God has promised to those who love him (James 1:12).

In some parts of the world, a "test" is a special kind of contest. It refers to a match between teams representing two nations. Since each country selects its best players to represent it, to be chosen for a test match is a great honor.

Sometimes God may select you for a test. He will let you get into a difficult circumstance in which your faith in God and your commitment to serve him are tested. Unlike athletic contests, these test situations are not something you look forward to with pleasure and excitement. You will have to make difficult decisions, to endure some hurt or pain or suffering, or to sacrifice something that is dear to you.

Yet James encourages us to meet such trials with joy. For to be tested by God is an honor. It means God thinks there is something in us worth being tested. A person without faith has nothing to test.

Furthermore, God's tests are a means of developing our faith. Passing the tests of life leads us to new levels of opportunity and experience in the Christian faith, and we grow stronger in the process. Paul says these tests lead to steadfastness and hope. James says among the results of being tested is patience. The virtues that belong to a Christian life become a part of us as we meet the tests.

Thus, because God wants our faith to grow and be strengthened, he may give us tests that are increasingly more difficult. In a sense this could be compared to the trial heats a runner must go through in order to be eligible for the big race.

We don't have to be afraid of failing future tests, however, because God has promised he will not test us beyond our ability. And we are assured that eventually the tests will lead us to the crown of life: eternal glory in God's presence. God has promised to give us the strength we need to meet and overcome the tests of life. And at the end of the course he gives us the award he has long before prepared for his people.

28

Superstar

With the LORD on my side I do not fear. What can man do to me? (Ps. 118:6).

Does your team have a superstar? Someone so good that when he or she is playing, your side always wins? If this one player is missing, you're likely to lose. This is the player who breaks every record in the book, and the opponents know they have no hope of winning against him or her.

Some barnstorming ball players travel with only part of a team, challenging local organizations. Their pitcher is so good, at least in comparison with the teams they play, that they really need only that pitcher, a catcher, and a few pick-up players to run bases and do some infrequent fielding.

The term *superstar* may not be fitting to apply to God. Yet, when he is on our side—or perhaps more correctly when we are on his side—we don't need anyone else. His presence brings the assurance of victory. "If God is for us, who is against us?" asked Paul (Rom. 8:31). Using a different figure of speech, someone has said, "One with God is a majority."

We need no one else. In fact, theologically speaking, no one else makes any difference. In our struggle against evil, only Christ contributes to the victory. Our efforts against evil are ineffective by themselves. ". . . all our righteous deeds are like a polluted garment . . ." said Isaiah (64:6). "Unless the LORD builds the house, those who build it labor in vain . . ." asserted the psalmist (Ps. 127:1).

Only Christ is capable of winning over sin. Yet he doesn't play the game alone. He includes us on his team and achieves his victory through us. He enters us, lives in us, and carries out his activity through us. You might say he allows us to carry the ball while he blocks out the entire opposing team. Weak though we may be, in Christ we become effective. "With God we shall do valiantly," sang the psalmist, "it is he who will tread down our foes" (Ps. 60:12).

In Christ we are "more than conquerors," not by our own capabilities but through him who loves us and exerts his power through us.

29

Lasting Power

And the hand of the LORD was on Elijah; and he
girded up his loins and ran before Ahab to the
entrance of Jezreel (1 Kings 18:46).

The first marathon runner was not a
Greek, but the ancient Israelite prophet Elijah! We
are told that this man ran from Mount Carmel, where
he had been involved in a dramatic confrontation
with the prophets of the idol Baal, to Jezreel. That is a
distance of from fifteen to twenty miles. Not only did
Elijah run that far, but the words suggest that he got
there faster than King Ahab, who was riding in a
chariot!

Why does this incident, interesting as it may be,
rate a mention in the biblical account of the prophet's
activity? Perhaps the answer is in the statement that
introduces it: "The hand of the LORD was on Elijah."
His remarkable feat is credited to the power of God. It
is thus an illustration of an assertion often made in
the Bible: when the power of God comes on us, great
things happen.

God's ability to accomplish remarkable results with us does not depend on our qualifications, but on his power. Jesus said, ". . . apart from me you can do nothing" (John 15:5). Paul asserted that God "by the power at work within us is able to do far more abundantly than all that we ask or think" (Eph. 3:20).

When the task demands more than we expected and we feel our strength beginning to give out, God gives us new power. Perhaps you have experienced what many athletes have: when you are nearing exhaustion you suddenly get a second wind. Those who believe in God declare that this new energy burst comes from him.

When we are faced with what may seem an impossible task, or when we are nearing exhaustion from a long, drawn-out struggle, the Bible tells us to "keep the faith." For it is not our strength but God's that matters. Paul goes so far as to say, "When I am weak, then I am strong" (2 Cor. 12:10b). In other words, when we stop thinking we can make the world over by ourselves and look to God to exert his power, things begin to happen. For his power is made perfect in our weakness.

30

Renewal

But they who wait for the LORD shall renew their strength, they shall mount up with wings like eagles, they shall run and not be weary, they shall walk and not faint (Isa. 40:31).

Between rounds, the boxer is sponged, stimulated, rubbed—so that his strength can be renewed for the next round. During time-outs, basketball and football teams go to the water bucket to be refreshed. During a marathon, the runners periodically suck on a sponge to get water and vitamins to give them more energy.

Even in studying we have to take time off once in a while or our efforts won't be very effective. In any prolonged effort, periodic renewal is necessary for success.

Such renewal is also needed in our spiritual lives. If we try to go through life without stopping, relying only on our own strength and resources, eventually we wear out. We begin to act hastily and often foolishly; we make unwise decisions and mistakes;

our performance becomes unsatisfactory. We become discouraged and may give up completely.

How can we be spiritually renewed? The Bible counsels us to take time to be in the presence of God, who is the source of the power we need. Thus regular worship is a vital part of Christian living. We need to take time for prayer, to stop our usual activities and listen for God's directions. We consult his message of guidance, advice, and inspiration in the Bible. By reviewing what God has done and the promises he has given us, we find encouragement to go on.

Jesus gave us an example. Especially before important decisions or crucial events, Jesus went off by himself to spend time alone with his Father.

God promises that he will renew our strength. The prophets say that those who let God refresh them are like the eagle—the seemingly tireless bird that climbs with effortless ease to heights far beyond human reach.

With the renewing strength available from God, we are enabled to rise above the problems that confront us. We get new strength to continue our course, no matter how arduous it may be.

Paul calls on us to be transformed by the renewal of our minds. This happens as we turn ourselves over to God so that we shall know and can carry out God's will. Then we shall declare with Paul, "I can do all things in him who strengthens me."

31

A Lasting Prize

> . . . Now they do it to obtain a corruptible crown; but we an incorruptible (1 Cor. 9:25, KJV).

Many high-school athletes are primarily motivated to excel in sports by the prospect of winning a college scholarship worth thousands of dollars, or even a contract with a pro team.

The athletes of Paul's day had no such dream. They were amateurs in the real sense of the word. If they won, they received no prize money, no lucrative contracts for endorsing breakfast food, no guest appearances on TV—not even a silver trophy to put on the shelf. Their prize was a crown made out of laurel leaves.

But for them this was enough. It symbolized achievement and victory—superiority. To wear a laurel crown was a high honor.

No doubt there were some who thought it wasn't much of a prize for their efforts. Similarly, some people today regard the rewards of a Christian life as of no more value than a wreath of perishable leaves. Some

89

contemptuously dismiss the goal of Christian faith as "pie in the sky, by and by."

But Paul insists that the rewards awaiting the Christian far outshine the most glamorous trophy. The prize given to believers is far more valuable than the richest playing contract.

Prizes awarded to athletes today may not wilt as quickly as a laurel wreath. But they still disappear disappointingly soon. You may get a million-dollar contract—but "you can't take it with you."

The Christian reward, on the other hand, makes life worthwhile now, and it lasts forever. Paul describes it as being incorruptible: nothing can spoil it. For Peter it is an "unfading crown of glory" (1 Peter 5:4): nothing can diminish its value or cause it to lose its luster. It is kept in heaven for you. Nothing can take it away from you.

This reward, won by Christ, is ours—not because we have captured it by our stellar performance, but because Christ, our champion, has given it to us.

The treasure God gives us is valuable beyond any human accounting. It represents the expenditure not simply of money, but of the precious blood of Christ. And it brings benefits now and forever that can't be bought.

That's a prize worth winning, for it is "the crown of life" (James 1:12; Rev. 2:10).

32

The Race Is Finished

I have fought the good fight, I have finished the race, I have kept the faith. Henceforth there is laid up for me the crown of righteousness, which the Lord, the righteous judge, will award to me on that Day, and not only to me but also to all who have loved his appearing (2 Tim. 4:7–8).

The race is over, and you've won! Now comes the glorious moment when the judge or official announces your name and presents you with a trophy. This moment makes all your strenuous training worthwhile. You're glad you kept at it, no matter how exhausting it was.

From his many references to races, it seems probable that Paul had often witnessed such a moment of high honor when the winner was awarded the laurel wreath and received the applause of the crowd.

Now Paul says that just such a glorious moment awaits all of us who love Christ. The award is ready for us now. It has been set aside for us, inscribed with our names, before we finish the race. For the prize has already been won, not by us but by Christ. He has run the race on our behalf; he has won the victory we are unable to achieve. Now as the Judge—the Righteous Judge—he presents it to us.

Perhaps Paul meant to contrast this Judge with earthly judges he had seen. You can no doubt recall instances when you felt the officials made a wrong decision. That happens with human judges. But Christ's decision is always right. And his decision is to give us the prize.

The award he gives is not just a wreath of laurel leaves, nor a trophy to be admired as it sits on a shelf. He gives us a crown of righteousness.

Is this ultimate prize worth the long and difficult struggle you must go through in your life? Think of what it means. This is not just a crown that sits on top of your head. It is an award that affects your whole being through eternity. You are made righteous—like Christ. He permanently changes your condition.

No longer are you sinful and weak, unable to win any race, or even to make a good showing. Now you have been given the power and perfection of Christ. You join other believers who become winners in the Lord.

What a glorious finish to a difficult race!